EXISTENCE OF GOD
Aquinas' Five Proofs

CHRISTABEL N. PANKHURST

B.A.hons Divinity. P.G.C.E.R.E.

QUEEN OF ANGELS PUBLISHING
SKIBBEREEN, CO CORK, EIRE

Published by Queen of Angels Publishing
Cappanabogha, Leap, Skibbereen.
00353 (0)28 33341.

ISBN is 1442164786 and EAN-13 is
9781442164789.

Cover design: By Siobhan Pankhurst

www.teachthefaith.info

www.queenofangelspublishing.org

DEDICATION

For Ian for Ever.

Saint Thomas Aquinas
Malta

CONTENTS

NOTE TO THE READER.

The reader may find it helpful to keep the following in mind. The proofs for the existence of God, are very simple to understand. However when knowing these proofs it is sometimes difficult to give a good account of them in a discussion with non believers. Non believers in the main would love to believe, for God writes His name on every human heart.

When reading this book take time to meditate on these philosophical truths, for this book is not presented as light reading.

The author introduces many technical and theological terms that the reader may not recognise. To aid in understanding, the author has provided a glossary of terms in the first few chapters. The reader may find frequent use of this list helpful as he or she reads, *Existence of God.*

CHAPTER I

CATEGORIES OF UNBELIEF

I once watched a man, slam his fists down on the table in front of him and shout, "There IS no God!" In a later conversation the same man expressed the belief, that human souls reside in the stomach. On another occasion he was heard to wonder in real awe, how a carrot knew how to grow, in just the same way all carrots grew!

It is hard to categorise this gentleman as an **atheist** for although he did hold to the theory that God does not exist, he still believed in the soul. The soul of course is spiritual. His beliefs are confusing and somewhat at variance with each other.

The term, atheist was often used as a derogatory term. It was used, as an accusation against Socrates, who did not worship the pagan gods of his day. On the other hand early Christians were known as atheists, because they denied belief in the Roman gods.

One of my friends who spent many years as a religious, does not believe in God, does not believe in the soul and insists that when 'you are dead, you are dead'. He indeed is an atheist because he categorically denies the existence of a spiritual First Cause above or outside the world.

I have many other friends who when asked, "Do you believe in God," will answer,
"mmm..well I think there is…… something."

This cagey reply was dealt with way back in the 13th century when Aquinas said,
"To know that God exists in a general and confused way is implanted in us by nature…This however is not to know absolutely that God exists just to know that someone is approaching is not the same as to know that Peter is approaching even though it is Peter who is approaching"

The word **agnostic** is another label that identifies people with no faith of any kind. An agnostic does not accept the existence of a supreme being. To this he will add, "And no one can prove there is a God."

'Agnostic' comes from the greek word for *knowing*, which was coined by Professor Huxley in 1869. He used it to describe people who regard as futile any attempt to acquire knowledge of God.

Recently I met a real live **Pantheist.** I was extremely shocked when this very sane, up to that point sensible person, pointed to a tree and told me it was God. I do not mean, in any way, to undermine the person concerned, and so I will explain how they arrived at this particular description of God.

Pantheism first emerged in the 18th century. The belief takes its name from the Greek god, Pan. The belief either supports the existence of many gods or as this person was advocating that the whole of the universe is the manifestation of God. In other words everything you see is god. This is an occult belief system which leads to the glorification of Man. It is logical to assume that if a tree is god then also is man. However on an average, man lives about 70 years, dies and is buried deep in the ground.

Of course this is not the type of God we intend to prove. We are seeking a transcendent God.
In all its forms Pantheism springs initially from three main types in which new cults base their thinking.

Firstly: there is the purely materialistic which says that matter is the only reality. What you see and touch and hear. Thoughts and reflections for them are only an organic process, they deny any higher moral value to rules and regulations. These values or lack of values now permeate social thinking. They spearhead the modern trend of the politically correct. The concepts of love and kindness sit uncomfortably with them and so we see how the caring professions in our society are slowly denuded of their altruism.

Secondly: there is the type who make the mind the only reality. This holds that the universe is only an idea; that God is an all embracing mind or idea constantly evolving itself into passing phases or expressions of being and attaining self consciousness in the souls of men. From this ideology one could conclude that a mass murderer is on the same level as a gentle innocent child. The acolytes of this belief system often profess to advancing towards becoming gods themselves. Here once again we see mankind worshiping himself.

Thirdly: there is the type that tries to steer a middle course that would hold neither mind nor matter to be dominant, God in this case is viewed as a 'double-faced' single entity.

Pantheism makes good bedfellows with all the new age ideas that flood the market; advocates of the New World Order, people in powerful positions who are pushing for a "One World Religion." Their advocates will announce, "We must rid the world of God, for it is religion that causes all wars". All these ideologies have one thing in common. They categorically deny the existence of a spiritual First Cause above or outside the Universes.

The above belief systems are earth bound in their ideology. They do not transcend the material element. When they do however seek to experience something beyond the physical realm they head out into an unchartered spiritual world. They are easy pickings for negative forces that appear to them as *angels of light*. These folk are easily recognised; they will view religious objects with contempt but hang a crystal in the window, change their beds around, insist on a plant in the corner and accept without query any new fad that pertains to come from a shaman.

Sadly there are the folk who don't like God overmuch and instead prefer Lucifer as their god, calling him the bright morning star. I have no intention of advertising their convictions.

None of the above can logically adhere to Christianity, but to the detriment of this faith they frequently do.

However when we regard the opposite stance from a Theist prospective we understand how narrow is the vast divide between them! Here is how Augustine of Hippo (354-386 AD), explains the God in and through all, yet outside all:

> "...He is a profoundly hidden God yet everywhere present; He is essentially strength and beauty; He is immutable and incomprehensible; He is beyond all space yet fills all the universe; invisible yet manifest to all creatures; producing all motion yet is Himself immovable; always in action yet ever at rest. He fills all things and is ircumscribed by nothing;   He provides for all things without the least solicitude; He is great without quantity therefore He is immense;   He is good without qualification, and therefore He is the Supreme Good"

It won't be until around 1265 that Aquinas will set out a full-proof method of scientific enquiry into the Proof for the existence of a God that all logical men recognise.

We often find that people who believe in a God when told that there are five proofs to support their belief, become highly insulted. Their faith is enough they say. This is not such a good idea, for we often find in life, that what we firmly believe at one time, we may come to view in a totally different light when we have more information or experience. In proving the existence of God we will use logic and science.

Lastly there are the many people who have asked me to write this book. People of differing faiths and people with none, they have one thing in common.

They have an open and inquiring mind.

CHAPTER ll

THE BASIC ARGUMENTS

There are five proofs for the existence of God. These proofs have nothing to do with faith, they are logical proofs that have stood the test of time.

We will first look at a brief outline of the concept of each proof. Then we will examine in greater detail the evidence that substantiates each proof.

In todays world there is a sense of hopelessness. There are very few monarchs left in the world to care about 'their people'. Most countries are ruled by an array of people no better or worse than those they govern.

At one time belief in God was natural when people had kingship as a reference. But beginning with the French revolution there was a dedicated, systematic long term plan to erase kingship from the world. Kings and Queens of Europe were Christian and the people followed their role model. They were seen by Christians to rule in God's stead. Those advocates of Godlessness and immorality assassinated the tzar of Russia and his family.

Communism crept seductively across the world.

If you are a Christian you need to know that the Jesuits when instructing converts from communism always began with these proofs for the existence of God.

The First Proof is taken from the idea of an Un-Caused Causer. The Cause of all, Himself uncaused. **This is that which we call God.**

The Second Proof is taken from the Un-Moved Mover. The source of all movement, Himself unmoved.

This is that which we call God.

The Third Proof is taken from possibility and necessity. A Necessary Being, for everything comes and goes, only He is necessary. HE IS.

This all mankind calls God.

The Forth Proof argues from the multiplicity to the One. For there is only a little good, a little love, in all of us and in all things. This must come from a Being who is all good, all love. HE IS all in ALL.

This we call God.

The Fifth Proof is taken from Design and is the most comprehensive of the five proofs. It also scientifically controverts Darwin's theory of evolution showing it to be impossible. The great designer or cause of design is,

That which we call God.

We will be making *metaphysical* examinations of concepts and need therefore, not just to understand this science, but also the theory of *truth*.

Tip: It might be simpler to read the Fifth proof first. Also these Basic Argument in this chapter, should be paraphrased by the reader in his own words and learned by heart

CHAPTER III

TRUTH

Today the nonsensical "everyone to his own truth" has become an accepted truth in its own right. Liberalism says to the masses, go ahead believe anything you want because that will be your truth and that is all that is important. There is a reason why liberals do this, but we haven't the space here to discuss their agenda.

Let me quote a great man of our time, Archbishop Marcel Lefebvre. He says:

> "In this view, liberty is based on dignity,which gives it its *raison d'etre*. Man can hold any error whatever in the name of his dignity. This is putting the cart before the horse. For whoever clings to error loses his dignity and can no longer build upon it. Rather, the foundation of liberty is truth, not dignity. "The truth will make you free,"(An Open Letter To Confused Catholics)

If someone views a blue colored vase and says, "This vase is all blue in color." he believes he is telling the truth. However if on turning the vase around he discovers that it has a red motif painted on the other side, then he must admit that, his first statement is not true. He may be above blame but no matter how sure he was that his statement was true, cannot make it true, if it wasn't.

In examining the proofs for the existence of God we need to leave aside this modernistic tampering with the ideals of truth which seeks to nullify the existence of Ultimate Truth. We need to genuinely investigate the concept in itself.

To do this we examine the three types of recognised truth. Logical truth, Moral truth and ontological truth.

Logical truth.

Logical truth is when a true statement is made that is acceptable: For instance: Paris is the capital of France and the battle of Hastings was fought in 1066. Both these statements are true, and the thought of the judgement behind them, is also true. With logical truth there can be no argument because statements are based on reality that is obvious to everyone. The Five Proofs are based on Logical truth.

Moral Truth. - Telling the truth.

This is the one most of us have a problem with because to be able to tell the truth we need the support of what is known as 'Virtue'. The virtue of Prudence is for deliberating, or taking counsel about what is to be said or done. Prudence strikes a balance when one is faced with conflicting demands or situations.

The virtue of Charity, requires that we love others enough not to steal the truth from them by telling them lies.

The Virtue of wisdom, teaches us that the telling of lies makes us physically stressed, which can lead to illness. In order for society to function properly we must be able to trust that what we are told is the truth in any given situation. This is why when governments lie or steal from their country the fabric of society is fractured and people loose hope.

Ontological truth.

Ontological truth is about things in themselves being ascribed the value of truth. We say that 'a man is a 'true friend' when he acts in a way in which we think a friend should act. The statement 'running true to form.' means the horse is acting 'true' to the behavior normally expected of it. First and foremost, truth is to do with what we think about things. We can see from this that truth is attributed primarily to the intellect and our thoughts.

Usually our truth is only partial. e.g. we can say many things that are true about the sun. We know it provides the light and energy that sustains life on earth; that it is made of hydrogen and helium. Scientists tell us that the sun's energy is from nuclear fusion reactions, in its interior. But there is so much more knowledge that is true about the sun. Knowledge that we have not yet gleaned. We cannot deny the possibility of many other truths about it.   This ontological truth will build our understanding of the attributes of God, once we realise that the existence of God can be proved.

CHAPTER IV

METAPHYSICS

The word 'metaphysics' was first used as a label to indicate the works of Aristotle which were put after the physics, or philosophy of nature. The philosophy of nature deals with limited classes of beings. Physics deals with things that move and can be quantified. A tree, a rock, the sun, the sea and the stars. Blood cells, radioactivity. In other words the natural world around us.

Father Francis Selman in his book
"From Physics to Metaphysics" explains:
> "Physics tells us how things act but it does not t e l l us why they exist. Metaphysics is about the most general causes of things existing; and so it is about what makes anything be." (page 5)

The sun, moon and stars do not know that they exist. We know that they exist and that we exist. Our minds are constantly seeking after the truth. We want the truth of why things exist. Scientist examine the reality of existing things. This is Physics. Metaphysics on the other hand is the Science that contends with the problems presented when we ask why?

If someone asks you the question, 'What is your philosophy in life?' You won't say, " Well I wash the car on Saturday morning and I bake cakes on Wednesday." No, you are aware they want something more from you. You realise that you will have to move away from the physical things you do and reflect on why you do them. This is what Metaphysics is about. It reaches beyond the physics of the known world and seeks the unknown.

Metaphysics is about finding out the cause of things. It is in endeavoring then, to make our implicit knowledge of God explicit that we use the science of metaphysics. A science, which deals with the source of all things and the ultimate principles of Being.

When we move beyond nature and into 'metaphysics' seeking the Cause of Light we deal with being that is beyond limitation or qualification, with being considered in itself, simply as being.   Isolating the concept of somethings '*thereness*' will become important as we read on.

Epistemology,
Epistemology is the name given to the Science of Knowledge. Epistemology is part of Metaphysics.
To try to understand the essence of being, whether of rock and rain or sunfish and sea we need knowledge. Our own simple knowledge will do. But to test out our knowledge. To evaluate it. To quantify it. We need another science.

If we are to arrive at any sensible conclusion in our quest to prove there is a God, we need to be able to trust our knowledge. It needs to be a science.

A Priori

A Priori is a term not often used in everyday language, but often used in philosophy. It denotes a concept arrived at from a process of mental reasoning or knowledge that comes from theory or deduction, rather than from observation or experience.

a posteriori

a posteriori means knowledge gained through witnessing the effect of things. Often it is called a demonstration: "a posteriori";

Summa

When the summa is quoted, the following abbreviations are normally used:

s.t. stands for Summa theologiae; Art. is Article and q stands for Question. The quotations used in this work have mostly been taken from that part of the summa entitled: Prima Pars Question 2 The existence of God.

Concupiscence

This is the word used to describe the strong desire in mankind towards satisfying the appetites of the flesh. Man is prone to sin in the flesh rather than to follow a spiritual life.

CHAPTER V

THE ANGEL OF SCHOOLS

The Five proofs for the existence of God were first formulated by Saint Thomas Aquinas who was born in 1225 A.D.

I was first introduced to Saint Thomas Aquinas at the age of twelve when I attended Dominican College Fortwilliam in Belfast. We sang about him being 'The Angel of Schools.' However it wasn't until I attended Maryvale College in Birmingham that I came to appreciate the sheer magnitude of this man's intellect. In my own feeble way I will try to use Thomistic philosophy to introduce you to his Five Proofs for the Existence of God.

Saint Thomas was an Italian philosopher, and theologian. As a Dominican priest; you will see him referred to as the Angelic Doctor. Aquinas is regarded as 'the greatest figure of scholasticism.'

Scholasticism was the system of philosophy and theology taught in medieval European Universities. The studies were based on Aristotelian logic, and the writings of the early church fathers.

One of Aquinas' most important achievements was the introduction of the work of Aristotle to Christian western

Europe. Aquinas' works include commentaries on Aristotle as well as the Summa Contra Gentiles and Summa Theologiae.

A summa is a compendium of theology and philosophy used as a textbook in the schools during the Middle Ages.

Aquinas was one of those men who was born holy. Even as a child Thomas loved solitude and prayer and the practice of virtue. It is recorded that he was a witty child, and had from the beginning manifested precocious and extraordinary talent and thoughtfulness beyond his years.

At the age of ten Thomas was sent to University. One of the major subjects studied in Universities was rhetoric.

Rhetoric is the art of persuasive speaking or writing which uses speech in such a way that the listener has no option but to agree with the ideas of the speaker. In the same way one might hurry to finish the sentence of another speaker, rhetoric forces the listener or the reader to finish the others thoughts. And not only finish the thoughts but have no option but to agree with them. Rhetoric is a lost art.

At University, Thomas apparently had a hard time from his fellow students who because he rarely spoke, called him 'the dumb ox'. One day some students excitedly called him to the window to witness a donkey flying. When he ran over and looked out, they fell about laughing at Thomas' naivety. Thomas is reported to have told them:

"I would prefer to believe a donkey could fly than you would tell a lie." Obviously a very intense young man he believed that to lie, deeply offended God.

However when his master of studies at the university discovered Thomas' knowledge he said:

> "We call him the Dumb Ox, but he will give such a bellow in learning as will be heard all over the world."

Thomas went on to teach in the Universities of Rome, Paris, Naples and Bologna. In 1263 he came to London to assist at the general chapter of the Dominican Order.

When Thomas had first wanted to join the Dominican order his family were very much against it and so his two brothers captured him and locked him in the fortress of San Govanni. He was kept there for two years.

Thomas as a young man had dedicated his life to Our Lady and as such wished to keep his purity unstained.

Thomas' family did everything they could to destroy his vocation. On one occasion his brothers brought a beautiful lady to Thomas' bedroom and she proceeded to entice him to make love to her. Thomas having difficulty persuading her to leave grabbed a burning brand from the fire and chased her with it. When he was sure she was gone, Thomas knelt down and implored God to grant him integrity of mind and body.

He fell asleep and as he slept, two angels appeared to him. They told him his prayer had been heard. They then girded him around the waist with a pure white girdle, telling him:

"We gird thee with the girdle of perpetual virginity" Thomas later told a friend that from that moment on he never experienced the slightest movement of concupiscence.

Aquinas' biographers describe him as frequently being in deep meditative prayer. Prayer being the raising of the mind and heart to God. Thomas was often found to be in ecstasy and floating above the ground. On one occasion at Naples in 1273 after Thomas had completed his treatise on the Eucharist, three other priests saw him lifted off the ground and a voice which came from the crucifix on the altar said, "Thou hast written well of me, Thomas; what reward wilt thou have." Thomas replied, "None other than Thyself, Lord"

It is from within Aquinas' work entitled The 'Summa theologica' that we explore these proofs for the existence of God.

Aquinas scientifically arranged his work. Firstly by posing a question. For instance:

"Whether the existence of God is self-evident?" Next he made a numbered list of all the arguments against that question, calling them **"objections."** Aquinas' next paragraph would be sub-headed: **"On the Contrary"** and would be a short statement of his hypotheses. His next sub-heading would be: "**I Answer That**: This would be an in-depth but precise answer to the question. Then heading his following paragraphs with "**Reply to objection one....two...three**" etc. With further precision Aquinas would use logic and rhetoric to overcome all the preceding objections.

The Summa is made up of 38 Treatises, 612 Questions, subdivided into 3120 articles, in which about 10,000 objections are proposed and answered.

Anselm's Ontological Argument.
Although he did it with such precision Saint Thomas Aquinas was not the first to examine the existence of God.

Anselm was Archbishop of Canterbury and died 21st April, 1109. He put forward an argument for the existence of God in a poem, the 'Proslogium'. Anselm says:

God is "that then which nothing greater can be thought"

Anselm says that what exists in reality is greater than that which is only in the mind. So since "God is that than which nothing greater can be thought", He exists in reality. Anselm believed that it was not possible to *actually* prove through material existence, that there is a God.

The German philosopher, Hegel who died in Berlin in 1831 was fascinated by Anselm's argument. However back in the 12th century Aquinas was having none of it. He says:

> "I answer that, demonstration can be made in two ways: One is through the cause, and is called "a priori," and this is to argue from what is prior absolutely. The other is through the effect, and is called a demonstration "a posteriori"; this is to argue from what is prior relatively only to us. When an effect is better known to us than its cause, from the effect we proceed to the knowledge of the cause. And from every effect the existence of its proper cause can be demonstrated, so long as its effects are better known to us; because since every effect depends upon its cause, if the effect exists, the cause must pre-exist. Hence the existence of God, in so far as it is not self-evident to us, can be demonstrated from those of His effects which are known to us." (s.t. Q2.Art 2)

At Mass on the 6th December, 1273. Thomas was in deep meditation and lost in ecstasy. We can only assume that God revealed something important to Thomas for later that day he said he would write no more. When Father Reginald tried to encourage him to continue writing he told him: "I can do no more. Such secrets have been revealed to me that all I have written now appears to be like straw" He did not finish the Summa theologica.

Then Thomas prepared himself for death.

Pope Gregory X, had called a general council at Lyons and commanded   Saint Thomas Aquinas to be there.   In obedience Thomas set out walking in January 1274 but fell to the ground. Thomas received the sacrament of Extreme Unction.

Thomas died just after midnight on the 7th March in 1274. No modern philosopher can begin to work on the ideas of a Supreme Being without first using Aquinas' five proofs for the existence of God.

CHAPTER VI

THE FIRST PROOF

IS FROM MOTION OR CHANGE

In his first proof for the existence of God, Aquinas begins with the argument which uses the concepts of motion and change.

Aquinas acknowledges that from experience we realise that in the world around us we see motion and change everywhere:

> "There is motion in the world, as is plain from experience, but everything which is in motion is moved by another, and it is impossible to proceed to infinity, in a series of movers which are actually and essentially subordinated; therefore there exists a first mover which is moved of none, and this we call God."(s.t.q1art3)

If we reflect on the world we realise that in nature all things move, to become something else. Seeds move within themselves and become flowers, trees, shrubs, herbs.

33

We will look at motion; at movement; at what causes movement. We can search and with experience find that nothing moves itself. We can trace the movement back to discover the First Mover, or Prime Mover for, this is what men call God.

The meaning of Motion
In this instance 'Motion' is taken to mean, any transit from potency to act.

The word motion here is taken to have two meanings.
The first definition of the word motion is of course locomotion. The movement we have come to associate with cars boats and planes. Machines moved by energy. Energy provided by the wind, the sea, the burning of fuels.

However the other meaning of motion is the one we need for our quest to prove the existence of a transcendent Being. Motion in this concept signifies any transit from potency to act. In other words, the movement of becoming or changing.

The word potency is derived from the verb 'posse' to be *able* or to have power.

A baby can be a philosopher although he is not one yet, and is therefore a philosopher in potency; but when he has acquired philosophic science he will be a philosopher in act. A baby can be a teacher, although he is not one yet, and is therefore a teacher in potency; but when he has acquired the necessary education he will be a teacher in act.

We often talk of our potentiality to become something. Aquinas wants the reader to reflect carefully on the fact that things that move from one phase of their existence to another need to be propelled by something else.

He would also like us to consider that when something is stationary it cannot at the same time be moving. Although this is obvious it needs to be contemplated to come to the full understanding that a stationary thing cannot move itself.

Take a block of wood. It has the potential to become at least two other things. It can become a fire. It can become a table leg, then be a fire and then particles of ash blown on the wind. In all of these, someone or something is necessary to initiate the move or change.

When we see television news bulletins of great swathes of forest burning, often the commentary will include the reason the fire started. In every house fire the question will be asked, 'how did it start?'

There is always movement
Imagine a large ball bearing or billiard ball placed centrally on a flat table top. Both (to our finite minds) in complete inertia. Our knowledge a posteriori enlightens us to the fact that the ball cannot move itself. Until something or someone applies some sort of force to the ball it will not move.

Yet from another angle there is movement. Even if the ball on the table was never, actually touched, in a thousand years the ball would have moved and it would take archaeologists to dig through 'the passage of time' to find it. For the wood of the table legs would fall apart and in falling down the ball would move.

Therefore it seems that nothing is allowed to stay in inertia. All things change or are changed. We cannot conceive of anything that does not move and change. From the hardest rocks found in the earth to the stillest air on a summer day - move and change. For some reason they are incapable of staying still.

But is this true? Can we stretch our minds beyond what we know and try to imagine a space in the Universe where nothing moves. We cannot use a modern theory of a black hole because the scientists who conceived this phenomenon have explained its cause - a natural movement in the cosmos. So that will not do for our investigation. Remember we are seeking something that does not move. When we find it we will call it God.

Let's imagine there was a place in the universe where nothing moves or changes. Just a few moments contemplating this possibility of looking into a large still space, we perceive that if there was anything at all in this space that never moved, someone or something would have had to 'move' it in there. Or, if the space was empty someone or something would have had to clear the space, in the first place. The only other possibility is that all things fell around the space and it itself was formed by the movement of other things passing it by.

Infinite Series of Movement?

An argument <u>against</u> this proof could be this: "It is impossible to find the first thing that moved because you can trace things back and back ad infinitum - in other words for ever. Movement is just infinite - always was and always will be." Watch how this argument is overcome.

We most often use the word infinity to describe that which has no limit, no end, and cannot be measured. Generally it is applied to space and time.

Philosophical concept.

Infinity is a word often used around descriptions of God. So in order not to short change the reader we will include a little philosophical brain gymnastics to ponder on:
Infinity denies all boundaries which are themselves negations. It is a double negation and therefore an affirmation in itself. It is said that it expresses positively the highest unsurpassable reality.

Infinity cannot be measured by adding to it, no matter how many times. Successive additions of it only renews its boundlessness. Don't be tempted to imagine infinity is nothing because although subtracting from it does not change it in any way it is still a positive concept.

Now the agnostic might argue the possibility that there is no Great Mover who started it all. Maybe movement is forever back and forever forward - Perhaps the movement is infinite. Forever we are immersed in a never ending never beginning ceaseless restless movement.

Why does the philosopher look for a first mover when all he experiences is movement?

Firstly, he sees that all things are 'caused' to move. As his intelligence leads him to ponder he realizes that there had to be a mover that wasn't in itself moved because movement must have a beginning and an end otherwise it is not movement.

For instance if we imagine a goods train which is infinite, i.e. that there is no beginning nor end to it. Imagine a train with so many trucks in it that the whole future is filled up with the trucks. Lets say the train has so many trucks it fills up the past also. That would make the train rigid and incapable of movement. But we know from our definition of infinity that it is impossible to 'fill it up' because it has no boundaries. So if the first cell came hurtling out of infinity and hit the boundary of the finite we would want to know who or what put it in motion. In a goods train each truck is moved and causes the action of the one immediately in front or behind. If the train is indeed infinite and no engine starts the movement then the train will not move. The train needs *something* or *someone* to move it.

Therefore, If we say, "There was no need for there to be a time to start the train because it (and indeed all movement) stretches back to infinity and forward to infinity", then the train will not move at all.

There is nothing known to man that just ups and moves itself. In a simpler way we see the same thing happening in a traffic jam. Let us imagine two roundabouts. For consideration we will take the Bandon roundabout and the Sarsfield roundabout with its little stretch of motorway in between the two. If traffic in Cork City was backed up from the Kinsale roundabout to the Sarsfield roundabout, and not one of the cars at the start or none of the vehicles at the end started to move, nothing would move.

Saint Thomas Aquinas explains:
> "Therefore, whatever is moved must be moved by another. If that by which it is moved be itself moved, then this also must be moved by another, and that by another again. But this cannot go on to infinity because then there would be no first mover" (s.t.art.3) … and therefore nothing would move.

In trying to find an explanation for motion without a cause we might contemplate the universe and observe that movement is more often circular. From the smallest particles of electrons and protons to planets and stars in the skies all move in circles that make their first mover invisible.

At this point into our minds might jump the picture of a train-set that runs around and around on the track. We might imagine that all movement is circular which would imply that there is no beginning and no end. But motion is movement, it still begs the question; how did it begin to spin? Nothing that we know of just ups and spins itself.

On the other hand lets consider the concept that things just are. That always there was spinning. Always. That the whole thing is beyond our comprehension. That there is no vocabulary to describe what we are really, experiencing here on planet earth.

Perhaps we should stop seeking, still our brains and accept. But that would entail defying logic and we are logical beings. It will also take us back to a time before Galileo and the understanding of the solar system. We will be forced to say the world is not really spinning and in need of a first cause, what we see is part of something else that we just don't know about. Will I contend that in this instance, this something we don't know about, **is that which we call God.**

But what if we have only part of the picture? That looking for a prime mover is useless as we do not have the full facts.

I remember watching my son feeding his Gecko. As soon as the little creature heard the lid being lifted on his aquarium he rushed out for the food. I recall thinking that this little lizard might imagine that my son was God and that Divine Providence had initiated the food from the 'sky'.

It struck me at the time, that maybe we had only a miniscule appreciation of what was really going on. Then I realised that in fact we do only have a very small part of the picture. We too, are very little creatures (most trees are taller than we are) who are dependent on others for the necessities of life. We don't live very long, three score and ten years if we are lucky. The most intelligent of our race discover ancient things about our world and act as if they created their newly found discoveries themselves. So my thinking came full circle, I realised that when the Gecko eventually evolved into a man he would see what we see and start looking for a prime mover!!

Remember we are looking for that First Mover, First Changer. When we find it we will call it God.
Lets return to logic and select any thing in the world and begin tracing it back to its beginnings. The modern mind influenced by the theories of big bangs or a large primeval soup arrive at the outer edge of the 'soup' and tip over into a black hole of nothingness! But, if we began with nothing then nothing would now exist. There would be no movement and no change.

In all things we need a first mover that is moved by no other. If we find something that started everything moving but was initiated by something else then we look for this something else, for it is the prime mover:

This Prime Mover, is that which we call God.

In search of the Prime Changer
Discovering a Prime Mover is no doubt easily enough understood but it is the concept, of Prime Changer that needs further interpreting.

> "But, nothing can be reduced from potency to a c t except by something in a state of act. Now it is not possible that the same thing s h o u l d b e a t once in act and potency in the   s a m e r e s p e c t, but only in different   respects" (s.t.art.3)

41

Simply put, anything that changes cannot change itself. The movement here is described as the passage from potency to act. No substance or material, can be in any given moment, both capable of action and carrying out the action, something has to work on the substance. For instance a standing boy, potentially can become a running boy but until his brain acts upon his muscles he remains in potency. So the same thing, in the same respect cannot be both in potency and in act.

> "Thus that which is actually, hot, as fire makes wood, which is potentially hot, to   be actually   hot, and thereby moves and changes it" (s.t.l.q2.art3)

From this can be comprehended that change is caused by something else. But we cannot go on to infinity as we have already seen above, otherwise there would be no change or movement at all.

If a piece of coal were placed on the burning wood, the coal moves from being potentially hot, to being hot by the actual wood which was made hot by the fire. Aquinas tells us that,

> "Now it is not possible that the same thing should be at once in act and potency in the same respect, but only in different respects. For what is actually hot cannot simultaneously   b e potentially hot, though it is simultaneously potentially cold" (s.t.l.q.2 art 3)

When an ice cube tray is filled with fresh water. That water has the potentiality to become ice. Water might become ice, but while it is water it is still water. Other elements have to be applied to it for it to change into ice. Water does not change itself into ice. All things are changed by something else.

Therefore the First Cause of Change, that itself has no Cause, is:

That which, mankind calls GOD

CHAPTER VII

THE SECOND PROOF

IS FROM THE NOTION OF EFFECTIVE CAUSE

The second way of proving the existence of God, treats the concept of 'cause' and in some measure 'reason', as being the pathway to understanding the first cause to be what everyone calls God.

Aquinas says:

> "There is no case known (nor indeed is it possible) in which a thing is found to be the efficient cause of itself, because in that case it would be prior, to itself. Which is impossible" (s.t.1.q.2art3)

An apple seed cannot cause itself. It did not bring itself into existence. A different apple seed caused it to form. And, a seed before that and one before that again. Tracing the apple seed back and back we can eventually arrive at a first cause. Can we go back past the imaginary soups, back past the big bang theory to one particle in which resided, all the knowledge of the world and the universes. This cell would need to hold all the information we have to date, and also all the information we have yet to discover. Can we look this tiny particle in the 'eye' and inquire, "And what caused you?"

Will it answer, "I was caused by that which has no cause, that which someday you will recognize as GOD.

Astronomer Fred Hyle has stated that believing the first cell originated by chance is like believing that a tornado ripping through a junkyard full of Boeing 747 airplane parts dismembered and in disarray, could produce a working 747 plane.

The world we experience has causes; not only of production of animal, vegetable or mineral but also of the conservation and endurance of the effects of the causes. In other words if they cease to act the effect will cease to be. This observable fact that everything happening in our living world can be traced to a cause scientifically proves that nothing can be self-caused because that would necessitate it, having to precede itself, which is not possible.

The philosophical argument is thus:
1. The scientific laws that govern the spatiotemporal universe (within time and space) show that everything has a cause.
2. Therefore the universe has a cause.
3. We call this cause the creator.
4. Therefore the creator is not subject to the causal laws that govern the universe.
5. Therefore the creator Himself has no cause.

For those who would argue that perhaps there is no first cause but an endless series of causes. Keeping in mind we are working from effect back to cause, and if one eliminates the first cause there will be no effect.

Therefore we take to the goods train again and realize that causes cannot be endless because there would be no first cause, no intermediate cause and no last cause - so there would be nothing.

But, we know from what we perceive that there is in fact, plenty.

It must be remembered that no matter what theory science proffers for the great beginnings. Whether it be a primeval soup, a big bang, evolution, or the most recent punctuated equilibrium, man must still inquire. "And, what caused that?" It is that first cause that we seek.

Remember we are not talking evolution here. We are not seeking the beginnings of man. We are looking back before that to the cause of all.

Science by its very nature can only find or discover what is already there.

However not all philosophers perceive cause and effect in the world as Post hoc, ergo propter hoc, some would argue that our finite minds might only be looking at a small part of the picture, a limited, length of time, with not enough experience in it for us to realise that the habits we see happening in our world might not continue. But this in no way substantiates a proof against a first cause for if we recall the Gecko we realise that no matter how limited the view, it still has causes and needs a first cause.

On the other hand scientists have discovered that effect does not always follow cause, that every so often something springs out of line for no conceivable reason. This has led many of them to declare that the 'no apparent reason' is that which we call God!
You see we are not, at present, saying anything personal about this, 'that which we call God'. We are identifying a FIRST, and naming this FIRST - God.

Being and Permanence.

Now we need to look to a superior cause in actual present operation.   Life on earth is dependent, on a certain atmospheric pressure in order for us to walk upon the earth without falling off. This pressure is dependent on the continual operation, of physical forces which depend on the position of the earth in the solar system. Spinning at 1,000 miles per hour the world is interdependent on many forces.   These conditions are continuously produced by definite constitution of the material universe. These fundamental principles cannot be self caused.   That they could cause themselves is impossible. For in order for it to cause, it needs to exist, which it cannot do until it is itself caused.

Acknowledging that the solar system and its attributes exist - and are not caused by themselves, they must be caused by another superior cause. If there were no first cause in operation on the solar system none of these dependent causes could operate either.

Therefore it is evident that the series of causes we are considering is not just those which stretch back into the past, in order to ascertain how the world began. We are not just looking for a definite moment that caused something to be, and moving in a series until the present day. In fact we are also considering an actual cause, now operating to account for the present being of things.

If this First Cause ceases to act then all will cease to be. We move away from becoming or change and consider further; being and permanence. Not all causes in the world produce something else. Many causes must act continually for the continual preservation of the world. That life on earth might be sustained their causes must be themselves caused by another.

That first cause is: **That which we call God.**

CHAPTER VIII

THE THIRD PROOF

IS TAKEN FROM
POSSIBILITY AND NECESSITY

In this third way we observe the dependence of existence, one thing depending upon another and the fact that these things do not necessarily need to exist.

In the first proof we considered beings as changing, or subject to change, in the second proof we looked at the cause of their actual existence. Now in this third proof we look at the fact that these beings do not need to exist. Nothing in this world or universe needs to be there.

All material beings, come into existence and go out of existence. Plants and animals come into existence and pass away. Chemical compounds, come together, form and again return to their original elements; as in the case of water and energy.

If things go in and out of existence it means that, they are not necessary. Don't be tempted to introduce to the argument of the necessity of the biology of the food chain because each series of organisms are dependent on the next and this would simply lead us back to First Cause and First Changer.

There was a point in time, when it was only a possibility, that each one of us might come into existence. Having now come into existence we will, some day, cease to exist.

To keep this flowering and dying in continuance there has to be a Being that of itself is necessary and permanent. It has to be there all the time to keep the show on the road.

We are forced to consider the existence of an Omnipresent being who, is not only present now, but always was present because, it is clear that, if at any precise moment in time, nothing had existed; nothing would exist now.

In contemplating the argument thus far, we realise that if these beings are not necessary then there was a time when none of them existed. Nothing at all existed, for none of these beings, of themselves, require to exist. Therefore when we reflect that if there was absolutely nothing in existence even a being who had the wisdom and omnipotence to cause existence then nothing could have happened. Our Universe, the stars, planets, our world, life on earth none of it would exist now.

It is clear that if there was a time when nothing existed, no First Cause, no First Mover then nothing would exist now.

Why then do contingent or unnecessary beings exist? They cannot do so by their own nature. By their own nature they are unnecessary. There is only one alternative, they must be produced by a being that itself is necessary. A being whose nature or essence is existence. This being all men call God.

Aquinas explains:
> "...we must admit the existence of some Being having of itself its own necessity and not receiving it from another, but rather causing in others their necessity.
> **This all men speak of as God** (St q1 Art 3)

A Being whose nature is existence itself.
It is in the **nature** of man to procreate. It is in the nature of mankind to love, to hope, to work etc. Also in the nature of man is death. In this way he passes out of **existence.** We need to reflect on the image of the *is* of existence. When we say something *is* there, we recognise something in existence. For instance, 'the bread is on the table' clearly means that bread, is in existence on the table. We use the term *is* to define a reality of **existence** in time and space.

Now let us look closer. Let us look at what makes up, the *is* of the bread. Fundamentally bread is wheat, water, oil, salt, sugar, and raising agent. The wheat is the product of a seed sown by man. Under a microscope the biologist will see that each of the ingredients are made up of millions of tiny cells. Each of them an **is** in its own right. We need to acknowledge that man makes bread (and every other thing) but he cannot create it. Man only ever 'discovers' what is already there. Man only ever makes something by gathering the components that already exist in the Universe and putting them together to make another *is*. Something that is now in **existence** that was not there before.

Man cannot create anything out of nothing. Man cannot even imagine a new *is* that has never been seen before. No man can draw a design for a space ship without using line and form, these already exist in the world. The most outstanding modern invention is the mobile phone, the idea for which was first formed (unknowingly) in the imagination of the inventor of the telephone many years ago.   Dreaming of converting acoustic vibration to electrical signals was a long shot but everything he gathered together in order to do it, was already there.

It is incorrect to say man invents anything. What he actually, does is 're-invent' or 're-cycle' the effects and the causes, that the First Cause created. Man as re-inventor passes out of existence so also does the material objects that he has brought together to make another *is*. On the other hand God *is* the *is* of always.

Each thing, animal, vegetable or mineral in existence has a different identifiable nature. Therefore it is logical to assume that the First Cause of these entities would not only have to incorporate all their individual natures but would need to transcend their sum total.

When we talk about '*being*' we refer to the concept of 'existence' i.e. the simple fact of existing, of being there to be seen, or heard, or touched. The first type of existence is qualified by quality or motion. Metaphysics on the other hand deals with *being* without any such limitation or qualification, with Being in itself, simply as Being.

To better explain we might think of a rabbit. The rabbit has existence. We can see him, touch him, watch him hop about and when startled sit up and listen for danger. He is *being* a rabbit. All these attributes make him recognizable to us as a rabbit.

When discussing a child's future we often ask a him, what does he want to *be* when he grows up.

To understand the essence of *being* it might be easer to contemplate the idea of 'a good friend'. Here we might mean, someone we grew up with and still hold dear. or it might be our dog, who watches lovingly by our side. The attributes of friendship are many but there is still something in our understanding of friendship, that is indefinably abstract. It is as if, when the word 'friendship' is formed, our minds move in pleasure at the conception, before we qualify why. It is that abstract part of 'friendship' that determines its character, this is its essence or nature.

Essence then is more often used as an abstract term. It is that intrinsic, indispensable quality of each and everything that determines its nature.

When we come to the Proofs for the existence of God we consider this essence in its most abstract.
In Modern Tominstic Theology, Professor Phillips says:
      "Such a consideration of naked being must
      clearly involve the greatest degree of abstraction

and the widest universalization of which the mind is capable, since to attempt to abstract further, i.e from being itself, would lead us to a contemplation of nothing."

We have already acknowledged that a necessary BEING, cannot be just the sum total of all contingent beings. For contingent beings do not have the reason for their existence in their nature. Recalling our rabbit the cause of his existence are mummy and daddy rabbit, however within his nature he does not have a reason to be there. How often have we heard the question, "Why am I here?" We intrinsically know we do not have the reason for our existence within our nature; we suspect something else holds the key to this mystery. On the other hand, a necessary BEING, omniscient, omnipotent and omnipresent, has in itself the reason for its existence.

So if the creatures in this world 'have not' the reason for their being in their nature, then we must conclude that: To add together an infinite number of 'have nots' will never make a 'have.'

Therefore any number of trees, rocks, stars, people cannot be the sum total of God. This agnosticism is what Pantheism erroneously believes and New Age thinkers advocate.
In this third proof we have been considering existence related to its essence, which is the very heart of metaphysics.
Here is how Aquinas Explains it:

"The third way is taken from possibility and necessity, and runs thus. We find in nature things that are possible to be and not to be, since they are found to be generated, and to corrupt, and consequently, they are possible to be and not to be. But it is impossible for these always to exist, for that which is possible not to be at some time is not. Therefore, if everything is possible not to be, then at one time there could have been nothing in existence. Now if this were true, even now there would be nothing in existence, because that which does not exist only begins to exist by something already existing. Therefore, if at one time nothing was in existence, it would have been impossible for anything to have begun to exist; and thus even now nothing would be in existence which is absurd. Therefore, not all beings are merely possible, but there must exist something the existence of which is necessary. But every necessary thing either has its necessity caused by another, or not. Now it is impossible to go on to infinity in necessary things which have their necessity caused by another, as has been already proved in regard to efficient causes. Therefore we cannot but postulate the existence of some being having of itself its own necessity, and not receiving it from another, but rather causing in others their necessity. (s.t. Q2.art.3)

This all men speak of as God."

CHAPTER IX

THE FORTH PROOF

ARGUES FROM
THE MULTIPLICITY TO THE ONE

The henological argument, is the philosophical term used to describe the forth way of proving there is a God.

We recognise, through our experience of the world, that all creatures have varying degrees of truth, goodness and nobility. The argument then goes on to prove that there must be a being who *is* absolutely Good, True, and Perfect.

My daughter helps herself with this one by simply saying, "yep, I got it. Its like, if there are three glasses of orange juice on the table there has got to be a big bottle of the stuff somewhere." However unlike the bottle of orange God does not deplete Himself.

Another way to visualise this might be to reflect on sunlight. If the day is overcast we describe it as a 'dull' day. Even in shade and shadow there are degrees of light.

However anyone who has flown in an aircraft will know that up above the clouds is the perfect light of the sun from whence all imperfect lights filters down to the earth. It is the graduation of the imperfect light working back to the perfect sunlight that helps us understand the argument.

However we must keep in mind that we can only work with concepts in the transcendental, that is, the non physical realm. We are only using sunlight and orange juice to grasp the concept on the metaphysical level.

Plato was the first to consider this argument. What he said was something like this: In the world things have more or less truth, more or less goodness, more or less being; the transcendental aspects of being are found in reality in a hierarchically graded order.

Plato was talking about metaphysics or things beyond the physical world being graded from the least up to the most.

When we talk about Truth, for instance, we see it as whole truth and nothing but the truth. However when we go looking for this truth we only find it in varying degrees in different individuals. Plato says that there must be a Being who had this truth in unlimited degree, in fact *is* this Truth. **And this we call God.**

In philosophical terms, "Multiplicity is inexplicable without a unity as its cause" Aquinas says:

> "If any one thing is found as a common characteristic in many things, it must be caused in them by some one cause." And of course, once again this is the cause we call God.

Not to be overlooked is the concept that truth, beauty, and nobility do not cause themselves in the individuals in which they are found. Just as the glass does not cause the orange drink to appear inside it.

If the glass falls and is smashed, we recognise in the splinters what once was a whole glass.

In a way we are taking all the degrees of perfection in the world and multiplying them together. None of these degrees of perfection caused themselves: What we get then is a massive amount of perfection which must be coming from a total amount of perfection. **This perfection we call God.**

There is another consideration in this proof, it has to do with the nature of something.

1. Any perfection such as love or nobility does not *imply* any *imperfection*.
2. When we say 'love' we are talking about a perfect concept, In 'love' there is no non-love.
3. Although 'love' in itself is perfect there are degrees of 'love'.

4. In some people there is a lot of this perfect thing called 'love'. In others there is very little 'love'. In other words there are degrees of this perfect thing called love.
5. Love is not part of man's nature. If it were then those who had 'no love' (for others) would cease to be human.
6. Therefore anyone having 'love' in a varying degree cannot possess it of his own nature.
7. And therefore must receive it from some 'other' which possesses this perfection of 'love' in its own nature.
8. This Being who possesses perfect love we call God.

> "Thus, like the three preceding arguments, it (the forth) rests on a fact of experience, for the interpretation of which we call in the principle of causality. It no doubt enriches the content of our idea of God considerably, by adding the attributes of unmoved mover, first efficient cause and necessary being; attributes which sound absolutely impersonal and even inanimate - those of Goodness, Truth, Unity, and fullness of Being or perfection. (MTTp2290)

What other attributes do we have in limited amounts that are drawn from the complete whole that we call God?
Let us consider the love a mother has for her child, or the concerned, personal interest human kind has for one another. What about communication, interaction,

emotion? If God contains the perfection of these human attributes then He is a personal God.

But we must not stray too much from metaphysics, Saint Thomas Aquinas explains that:

> "The fourth way is taken from the gradation to be found in things. Among beings there are some more and some less good, true, noble and the like. But "more" and "less" are predicated of different things, according as they resemble in their different ways something which is the maximum, as a thing is said to be hotter according as it more nearly resembles that which is hottest; so that there is something which is truest, something best, something noblest and, consequently, something which is uttermost being; for those things that are greatest in truth are greatest in being, as it is written in Metaph. ii. Now the maximum in any genus is the cause of all in that genus; as fire, which is the maximum heat, is the cause of all h o t things. Therefore there must also be something which is to all beings the cause of their being, goodness, and every other perfection; and this we call God. (Prema Pars   Question 2 Article 2)

The totality of Perfection is that which we call God

CHAPTER X

THE FIFTH PROOF

TAKEN FROM THE GOVERNANCE OF THE WORLD (DESIGN)

When we consider how a carrot grows and all carrots grow in exactly the same way we wonder how it 'knows' how to grow since the carrot lacks intelligence. The moon acts on the waters of the earth lifting them in such a way as to cause the tides. It continues to act that way although it also lacks intelligence. That small particle of life, a sperm is designed to swim for its life to an egg having no prior notion of its existence.

If Aquinas lived today wouldn't he have been ecstatic with joy at what science has discovered about the erudite Designer. That which he called God. He says:

"We see that things which lack intelligence, such as natural bodies, act for an end, and this i s evident from their acting always, or nearly always, in the same way, so as to obtain the best result. Hence it is plain that not fortuitously, but designedly, do they achieve their end. Now whatever lacks intelligence cannot move towards an end, unless it be directed by some being endowed with knowledge and intelligence; as the arrow is shot to its mark by the archer. Therefore some intelligent being exists by whom all natural things are directed to their end; and this being we call God." (Q2.ART3)

This proof can be broken down into four simple points:

1. We see that some things that lack cognition go on acting in the same way that is best for them.

2. We can deduce from this that it is not by chance but by intention they do so.

3. Therefore these things that have no knowledge must be directed by some being that has knowledge and intelligence.

4. Therefore their exists an intelligent being who guides and directs all things which they themselves cannot decide to do. **This Being we call God.**

Dr Jobe Martin

Dr Jobe Martin comes from a scientific and medical background. As an evolutionist he was in 1971 giving a lecture to college students in Dallas, on the evolutions of the tooth. He himself had been taught the theory of the big bang and believed that we ourselves started as a speck of light 600 million years ago. After he finished the lecture some of his students came to him and asked him "Dr. Martin, have you ever investigated creation science?"

They asked him to first study the assumptions made by evolution scientists, explaining that he would discover that these assumptions were not validated.

In the film, "Incredible Creatures that Defy Evolution" Dr Martin describes his disillusionment with the evolution theory when he came to the study of creation science. In the film he describes the unique design of many animals. One of these is the Bombardier Beetle

The design of the components that make up the body of the Bombardier Beetle

The Bombardier Beetle is a ground beetle half an inch long that makes little bombs within his body and fires it at an attacker blowing the menace away.

This beetle has been designed with a little chemical factory inside its body that manufactures bombs. The chemicals are stored together in a chamber and held in neutral until needed. If attacked the Bombardier Beetle releases them into another chamber before firing them out of his body. The explosion which blows even the biggest spider a good distance away comes out of twin firing tubes on the Beetle's body which he can turn around like a gun turret, back, front and both sides.

This creature must have been deliberately designed.

The Bombardier Beetle could not have evolved.

The first time the Beetle made the chemicals inside its body it would have blown itself up because it would not have known to evolve the two chambers.   A splattered bug cannot evolve.

Actually, the first time it concocted the bomb inside the second firing chamber it should have blown itself up. And splattered bugs don't evolve. The reason it doesn't explode is because it is designed with a specially lined firing chamber. This chamber could not have evolved because the bugs being destroyed could not evolve into the more complex bugs we know today.

Another interesting thing about this little fellow: When he fires the bomb, he himself doesn't get blown away by it. This is because although the human ear can pick up the 'pop' noise of the bomb exploding, scientists have discovered that there is actually one thousand little sequential bangs fired out so fast that it arrives at its destination as one large bomb.

Design and function are the main components of this proof for the existence of God. We who enjoy making and re creating so much - how can we deny the Glory to the Supreme maker and designer of all.

That which we call God

CHAPTER XI

THE ATTRIBUTES OF GOD

Having looked at the proofs for the existence of God we are ready to meditate in awe, the divine attributes.

Creation is a sort of mirror that reflects the divine perfections, thus from the beauty of things created we can infer the greater beauty of Him who created them.

So again from the order that prevails in the visible world we can conclude that He who made it is a Being of surpassing wisdom, and from its vastness we learn the power of Him Who upholds and supports it. Yet the knowledge thus obtained is always imperfect and obscure, we see through a glass darkly.

If you practice knowing the divine attributes especially the omnipresence and the omniscience, I can promise you a peace of soul beyond understanding. This is a type of mediation called 'recollection'.

This recollection can be practiced where ever we are or whatever we are doing. Saint Catherine of Senna remained aware of the Divine Presence in every moment of her life.

The Divine Attributes

If we recall how in chapter one, Aquinas said that

> "to know that someone is approaching is not to
> know that Peter is approaching even if it is
> Peter that is approaching" therefore having proved

logically that God exists we need now   to examine who God Is. What do we know about His Divine Essence?

The Catholic Catechism lists thirteen attributes or character traits of God. We will list them here and then choose a few to examine in the light of the five proofs.

To accept that God has these character traits we recall what was said in The Forth Proof for the existence of God, where we acknowledged the existence in man of goodness, mercy, justice etc. Now in God's attributes we consider the whole of knowledge, presence etc.

1. God is **eternal**, always was, is and ever will be.

2. God is **omnipresent**, He is in every place.

3. God is **immutable** He remains the same for ever.

4. God is **omniscient,** He knows all things, the past, the present, and the future, and also our most secret thoughts and actions.

5. God is **supremely wise**, He knows how to direct everything for the best, in order, to carry out His designs.

6. God is **almighty**, God can do all that He wills and that by a mere act of His will.

7. God is **supremely good**, He loves His creatures (us) far more that a father loves his children.

8. God is **very patient**, He allows the sinner time for repentance and a change of life.

9. God is full of **mercy and compassion**, He very readily forgives our sins when we are sincerely sorry for them.

10. God is **infinitely holy** He loves good and hates all evil.

11. God is **infinitely just,** He rewards all good and punishes all evil deeds.

12. God is a God of **perfect truth,** all that He reveals to man is true.

13. God is **faithful**, He keeps His promises and carries out His threats.

In the above list we have divided God's attributes or character traits. Human beings need do this in order to label and identify things. In fact, there is no division in God. Instead each attribute is total and perfect and one.

To better understand this, it might help to imagine a pot of white paint to which the colour yellow is added and stirred until it disappears into the white. If then the colour green is added and stirred until it too disappears into the light yellow and the paint takes on a blue colour, we perceive that each colour is totally throughout the paint without holding to individual colour definition.

God is eternal

With God there is no past or future it is all present with Him. With God there is no succession of events, there is no time with God. The whole history of the world, past present and future, is at all times in His sight.

God is Omnipresent.

All created things including ourselves exist in God (careful here, because a tree is *in* God does not mean the tree is God) To better understand this we might consider how a thought exists in our minds. The thought is real but small, our minds are bigger than the thought. No matter how many thoughts we have, our mind is still larger that the sum total of the thoughts. This is the same of God. All creatures exist in God, but He is not their sum total. He is larger than all that exists in Him. Otherwise He could not have caused them. We might decide to make a cup of tea, when we make it we don't become the cup of tea.

God cannot be contained in any way, in any space or in any idea we might have of Him. Our bodies are contained in space or they take up space.

Our spirits on the other hand are not contained in space, however our spirit can only be in one place at a time, unlike God who is everywhere.

The spirit does not reside solely in the stomach as the man in the first chapter thought. No the spirit or soul permeates all parts of the body and yet it is total in each part of the body. You cannot cut up a soul. If a man looses his leg, his soul does not become less.

Saint Bernard tells us:

> "God is everywhere yet nowhere. He is near us yet far away. All creation is in Him, and yet it is as if He were not in it"

Aquinas describes the omnipresence of God by explaining that,

> "First, as He is in all things giving them being, power and operation; so He is in every place a s giving it existence and locative power. A g a i n , things placed are in place, inasmuch as they f i l l place; and God fills every place; not, i n d e e d , like a body, for a body is said to fill place inasmuch as it excludes the co-presence of another body; whereas by God being in a place, others are not thereby excluded from it; indeed, by the very fact that He gives being to t h e things that fill every place, He Himself fills every place." (Q8.art2)

God in heaven is seen by the angels and saints. God has a special indwelling in the souls of good people by the power of the Holy Ghost. God is seen, adored, and loved by mankind here on earth in His presence as the God-Man in the Blessed Sacrament.

During my formative years I attended a small Protestant primary school in Co Antrim. We were taught that God was everywhere and we felt a happiness and security about that. We knew we were loved by this great Being who watched over us all the time.

Professor Phillips in the The Catholic Catechism Explained says:

"We ought therefore continually to bear in mind that God is always present with us" and quotes Saint Ephrem who says:

> "He who always has God in his thoughts, will become like an angel on the earth." (page 116)

God is immutable   The immutability of God moves us to a place of security and trust beyond the need for speech to describe it. God never changes. In such an uncertain world where we ourselves are the most fickle of creatures. We are suspended in a God that is constant. We savour this God who never becomes better or worse. Because God is perfect Truth `He cannot change. For Truth does not change otherwise it is not Truth.

God is omniscient God knows all things, the past, the present, and the future, and also our innermost thoughts.

This attribute of God is one of the most discussed and the least understood.

We go back to the forth proof where we gained knowledge of God's existence by looking at the smallest things in the world and searched out each ones perfect whole - that which we call God. If then we consider the eye of man who sees only dimly. Man can see and understand the grandeur and beauty of the world around him but needs to make a more perfect 'eye' of a microscope to see the things that exist that he cannot see, and which have always been there. As we lead our daily lives there is so much that we cannot see that is there to be seen. Why would we doubt that there is infinitely more in existence.

A telescope is made to see beyond our own universe. We now know that we can see thousands and millions of years past, as we gaze along the light of a star.

Why do the same scientists who spend their entire lives searching for what they think is there, at the same time deny the existence of something they have not yet discovered?

The creator of the eye, the creator of man's intelligence must therefore be able to see totally. Not just the present but for all history, past and present. For He is immutable, He is completely still.

Astronomers tell us that some of the stars we see are already dead, by the time their light reaches us.   If we can see into the past along the light of a star, how much more can the creator of the stars see?

One of the most amazing things in this world is **Divine Perspective.** All artists know about divine perspective. It is one of the skills they must master if their work is to look real. Children don't know about divine perspective. A child's first drawings will have everything in it the same size. Mum, dad, brothers sisters and the family home will all be represented on their page as being of equal size. As the child becomes more mature mum and dad will move to the front of the picture and a house will be seen smaller and further up the page giving the house which is in fact the biggest thing on the page, a new reality by being represented as smaller.

You can watch 300 people climb into a massive aircraft, when it takes off into the sky it becomes very small! It still has all those people in it. While it was on the ground and you were near it, you couldn't see anything else past it.

We take it for granted, in fact you probably think I am mad to even mention it.   But whoever designed divine perspective was very cleaver indeed.

Understanding The Omniscience of God
I will address the following aspect of omniscience because so many people who have some sort of belief in a God often cannot fathom how it works. God sees the things we will do in the future. He might see us do something really evil. That does not mean we have no option but to do this

evil. In the same way that we might see, from a distance, someone shoot another person. Because we see it in the distance does not mean the person is constrained to carry out the act. "God sees the deed because the man does it; the man does not do it because God sees it" (catechism p117) If a past action is in our thoughts now in the present, we know it wasn't caused to happen *because* we are thinking of it now.

If we think back to the already dead star we mentioned earlier; because we see the light of the star that died coming to us through the years into our present time; does not mean we caused the star to die.

If we have proved to our own satisfaction that this God exists it is now time to contact Him. Here are some reasons why:

People who report to have been in communication with Him, report favorable results.

It has been scientifically proven that those who are in communication with Him recover from illness more quickly than those who are not.

People who are 'found' by Him report never being alone.

People who are on friendly terms with Him do extraordinarily good deeds for others at the expense of their own comfort.

BIBLIOGRAPHY

Lefebvre Marcel Archbishop. *Open Letter to Confused Catholics,* Angelus Press. Kansas City, Missouri.2001

New Advent, Catholic Encyclopedia and Summa

Pieper Josef. *Guide to Thomas Aquinas.* Ignatius
    Press San Francisco. 1962

Phillips, R.P. D.D, M.A. *Modern Thomistic Philosophy. An Explanation for Students. Vol II Metaphysics.* London Burns Oates & Washbourne Ltd. Publishers to the Holy See. 1943

Selman Francis, Rev Father. *St Thomas Aquinas, Teacher of Truth.* T&T Clarke, Edinburgh. 1994

Selman Francis, Rev Father. *From Physics to Metaphysics.* The Saint Austin Press, 296 Brockley Road, London. 2001

Spirago-Clarke. *The Catechism Explained. An exhaustive Explanation of the Catholic Religion. A Practical Manual for us of The Preacher, The Catechist, The Teacher and the Family.* Tan Publishers Rockford, Illinois 1993

Venerable Louis of Granada (1504 - 1588) Tan. *The Sinner's Guide*. Tan books and Publishers, INC. Rockford, Illinois 61105

INDEX

19008612R00048

Made in the USA
Middletown, DE
30 March 2015